Heartways Press
P.O. Box 8118
Brattleboro, Vermont 05304

Cover Design by Judy Oliver
Cover Photo by Eleanor LeBlanc
Typesetting by Diane Conti

ISBN 1-879159-05-8

AVAILABLE LIGHT

POEMS

PAUL FERRINI

Table of Contents

Shiva's Embrace

We have argued to no avail
about our visions.
We have seen them as different
and struggled to join,
and we have seen them together,
only to find ourselves
moving apart.

Now love comes into the heart
without argument,
and the walls
that once stood between us
dissolve
in the raging current
of a love
we cannot begin to understand.

I close my eyes now
and feel the turbulence settle down,
revealing a face
that is all gentleness.
There is nothing here
that judges or rebukes,
but instead
a loving certainty,
that takes away illusion
only to reveal the truth.

It is 2:00 A.M. when we finally
go upstairs to the meditation room.
As you sing Bhajans,
the light in my heart deepens
and I hear your voices
as if for the first time.
Your call to Shiva
goes out through my heart,
though I do not suspect
He will answer it there.

He could have any body,
yet he chooses mine.
I do not understand why.
It is ironic, is it not?
I, whom you have seen
mercilessly tearing down
your defenses, have become
the one who comforts you now.

These arms that surround you,
reach to eternity,
yet the energy that lifts them
lifts you too.
Your complaint about me has gone.
Your physical distress
has dissolved.
Light has come to you tonight.
He has answered your call.

Tonight I am the father
who comforts and soothes.
And you are my daughters
welcoming me with songs
of uncanny beauty.

I know you understand
that I cannot stay.
I come to remind you simply
that you are loved,
even when you resist my embrace
and look to me
through your pain.

I have taken from you
all needs but one,
and I will take that one too,
if you will let me.
If there is any truth in your desire
it will be fulfilled.
If not, nothing you do
can force that fulfillment.

Hold me not,
and you will not miss me,
for I dwell with those
who find acceptance
at the edge of grief,
and love
beyond the reach of fear.

Towards a New Economy

I

If you have something to give,
offer it to others.
Do not wait for someone to ask for it.
The person who needs your gift
is approaching you.
If you do not offer what you have,
he will not recognize you as the one
who brings the gift he needs.

II

The law of supply is simple.
Those who give what they have
receive in full measure;
those who withhold it,
cannot enjoy it.

What you share
returns increased in value and scope.
That is what abundance means.
There is always more
of a good thing.

III

Offer your gift to all
regardless of their ability to pay.
Your purpose is to give,
not to evaluate the gift,
or to place conditions
on giving it.

What you do for others,
you also do for yourself.
What you do for yourself,
you do for all.
That is the working
of the golden rule.

IV

The world is fed by your labor in this moment.

Never forget: each one of us feeds the world
and is fed by it.

V

If you love me,
do not ask for what I cannot give
or what I can give only with difficulty.
Ask for what I can give freely.

Giving freely to you helps me release
what my fear holds back,
drawing to you gifts neither one of us
thought possible.

VI

The well is deeper than we know.

VII

A man must earn his bread,
but no one should tell him how to do it.
His survival is his responsibility.
Take that away, and take away his dignity
and his right to self-determination.

VIII

Men looked for gold
in the hills
instead of in their hearts.

They carried little pans
and chipped away
at the stones of earth.

They worked for money.
They lived for money.
They died for money.

And they left behind
angry witnesses
to their lives.

I can see them now,
these brothers,
looking for friends,
and I know
they would trade everything
for a single blessing.

IX

After the goldrush
I looked in my heart,
and saw that I was not happy.

I had found gold,
but it was a fool's gold.
It did not satisfy me.

Because I did not enjoy
what I labored at,
my labor was without energy
or value.

After the goldrush
I looked in my heart
and understood

that means and ends
must be congruent
for abundance to manifest.

X

Without happiness,
there is no abundance.

Happiness and grace
are the handmaidens
of the Infinite Supply.

One rests within me,
the other surrounds me.

XI

If a man does not do
what he wants to do,
he does not honor himself
as a man.

If a woman does not act
in accord with how she feels,
she does not honor herself
as a woman.

If a man does what he wants to do,
he meets the inner woman.
Then he understands the needs of others
and his work has meaning.

If a woman acts in harmony with her feelings,
she meets the inner man.
Then she knows the direction to be taken
and can act decisively.

When a man brings the inner woman forward,
he finds equality with his wife.
When a woman brings the inner man forward,
she finds equality with her husband.

This is the secret of the new economy.

XII

For years men have labored outside the home.
Leaving the home,
they left behind the integrity
of their feelings.

Without feelings, they could conquer,
but they could not contain.
They could subdue, but they could not endure.
Like grass that grows more quickly
when it is cut,

each intervention in the natural order
brings with it custodial demands
that restrict further growth.

No matter how hard men seek
to avoid the feminine,
they must meet it sooner or later.
All expansion is contained.
Every action
brings an equal and opposite
reaction.

Leaving the house,
man meets the feminine in the marketplace.
He sees the sword of the Goddess
but he does not understand
why it cuts away his pride,
his status,
his material possessions.
He does not understand
that it is all just an invitation
to come home.

XIII

For years men have labored outside the home,
missed by their sons and daughters.

Without the father,
the son is unsure of himself;
he moves without direction.
He lives in his mother's shadow,
or he retreats into himself
and becomes inaccessible.
Without the father,
the daughter does not feel appreciated
or protected;
she does not learn to take herself seriously,
becoming a target for abuse,
or she takes herself too seriously,
scaring men away.
The mother adjusts to the father's absence.
She enters the marketplace,
but she is not happy.
She does not want to do a man's work.
She needs to do her own work.

When the man returns to the hearth,
the home pulsates
with a hitherto unexpressed anger.
The man must walk through this anger
to embrace his wife
and to gather his children
into his arms.
Lest he do this, he cannot understand
why he is here,
nor the nature of his work on earth.

XIV

The new slavery
occurs when a man does not hear
the song of his own heart.

If he does not hear the song of his heart,
he cannot be a partner
in the dance of life,
nor can he be a father
to his children.

A man must walk through the woman's tears
to find his own.
He must understand his sadness.
His joy is born of grief.
His manhood is born
out of his capacity to feel.

XV

Only a slave is put to work
before he is ready.

XVI

When man and woman join together in spirit,
celestial beings are born.

They feed the hungry, cure the sick,
and uplift the hearts of all beings.

XVII

When the King of Cups approached, his consort
hid behind the nearest tree.

She became small like his daughter,
large like his mother;
she became all things to him,
yet still he called to her.

She did not want to give up her sword.
She fingered her necklace of skulls.
But fear did not arise in him.
Still he called to her.

Then she came to him,
for she knew he would not go away
until she joined him.

XVIII

Man brings the heart into mind.
Woman brings mind into heart.
The heart-mind
is the Creator of all things.

XIX

A man once told me:
"I have very little money,
but I have many friends."

He was a wealthy man.

XX

Living in the consciousness
of infinite supply
is not
as easy as we think.

Famine is a condition of minds
agreed on sacrifice.
Almost everyone
is dying
of some kind of hunger.

XXI

When you love someone,
you give without thinking.

XXII

The first law of Being
is to feed the hungry.

Those with roots in the earth
understand this.
Those without roots
are suffering
from a different kind of hunger
that cannot be appeased
until everyone has been fed
and welcomed with love.

XXIII

Greed and poverty go hand and hand.
One takes what he does not need.
The other resents him for it.

XXIV

If money is shit, as Freud said,
it is only because we give
leftovers.

When we give the best we have,
We begin feeding each other.

XXV

Love is the philosopher's stone.
It transmutes
and purifies all things.

Experience is base metal
and slowly turns to gold
as each person stands
for the truth of what he is
and releases the impurity
of what he is not.

Life is the fiery furnace
dissolving every false idea,
every untrue feeling,
and mixing the metals
that remain.

You see, we are learning how
to make gold
in the heart,
and we know now that this
is the only occupation
there is.

XXVI

I used to think in terms of buying and selling.
Now I know all that is illusion.
No one owns anything by himself.

Everything I have was given to me
that I might find the light in it
and pass it on.

XXVII

It is impossible to legislate fairness.

Fairness arises from equality.
I cannot play fair with you
unless I know in my heart
that we are equal.

Systems of weight and measure
promise fairness,
but lead to an unequal distribution
of the world's resources.

That is because they are created
out of the consciousness of lack.

When we are concerned about
what we will receive in return,
we cannot give the gift we have.

Concern for money or resources
is always fear based.
It doubts the inner gift,
prevents it from being offered to others,
and so interrupts the manifestation process.

As long as I am giving,
I am giving to myself.

As long as I am giving to myself,
I am giving to you.
Only when I stop giving
do I need to keep tabs
on what I get.

Calling you to account
for what you are giving to me
is just a devious way
of bringing myself to judgment
for not trusting my gift
and sharing it with you.

The pendulum swings both ways.
What I give
or refuse to give
always returns to me.

XXVIII

Abundance comes from what is present,
not from what is absent.
We see what we value
and expand it where we find it.

If what I value I see outside of me,
I will keep it there.
If I know it is already present
in my life,
I can embrace and quicken it.

I cannot create what I do not have.
But what I have
I can amplify and extend.

The creative source of my being
does this effortlessly.
I need only trust it.

My wealth abides in the heart.
It does not exist in external things.
If I am happy, I cannot be poor.
Trusting my happiness demonstrates this.

XXIX

The law of scarcity is simple:
the more I think about
what I do not have
the more I miss it.

If I look to you to supply
the food I believe I lack
I will always be hungry.

I must learn to feed myself.
Only then can I allow you to feed me.

XXX

The only food is love.
I cannot feed the world
if I do not feed myself.
But if I feed myself
by taking food out of your mouth,
I am a glutton for punishment.

XXXI

By my labor is the world fed.
By my labor of love is the world loved.

Love is my only supply.
Love is the only gift I have to give.

Wherever I live is love's house
made manifest.
Whenever I receive nourishment of any kind,
I receive the holy sacrament,
the body of Christ.
Whatever I do in each moment
is the work of the infinite mind,
whose plan of love I intuit
and carry forth.

You whom I love are the divine beloved.
You have come only to bless me, Kali,
Goddess of the Heart.

You have shown me the face
behind the face I fear
and it radiates only compassion.

I am your Son,
and I am not ashamed
to be nurtured at your breasts,
nor am I afraid to depart from you
to attend to my Father's work.

I inhabit the bliss body
of the Father/Mother.
I am the radiance of their joining.
I am the understanding of their eyes
and the gentleness of their touch.
My essence is love.
My coming and going is
full of grace.

Whatever I do is an opportunity
to bless and be blessed.
Everything else is the economy of fear.

I have made the choice.
I have chosen Love's economy.
I have chosen not to look for wealth in the world,
but to find it in my heart.
I have entered the house
of my divine parents,

and they have honored me
and made me welcome.
As long as their love is with me,
I shall not be homeless,
nor want for anything I need.

For Love blesses
and Love provides.
Love refuses no one
nor can anyone
refuse to be loved.
Love is the only currency
outside fear,
and in Love's embrace,
the images of fear
fall away.
All forms of scarcity,
all need to control,
all desire to manipulate,
all compulsion to know
or to figure out,
fall away from us
and dissolve in the flames
of Love's presence
in our lives.

The Approach of the Bride of Light

I

I do not recognize her form
but her eyes sing to me.
I ride them like stallions
back to a time
before the sacred vessels
were broken,
before the sacred songs
were cast off in the wind.

I ride on a saddle of leaves
into the silence of dusk.
I ride the minutes
of her coming and going,
drifting through the sounds
of bodies entwined on a dusty bed.

I linger at the water's edge,
in the shadow of the buffalo.
We have been here before
in a different time. It was then
passion was made radiant.
Now a smile lingers.
And I guard the burial ground.

II

It is a sad time.
It is a time without understanding
or conscience.
It is a time of fear
and the acts of fear.

Bodies are taken down in the field
without a prayer for their souls.
The animal has not been thanked
for his sacrifice.
Wild fruit dies on the vine.
The old ways have been forgotten.

III

Out of the darkness of night
the bride of light comes,
her aura ablaze
with shades
of rose and turquoise,
a shimmering white arc
slowing the steps taken
in fear.
She arises within
before she manifests without.
That is the only reason
you could come here

wearing her headdress
of crystal and eagle feather.

Others too are being drawn
and soon will be
gathering with us.
Her tribe is assembling
at the vortex of light.
Soon there will be many hearts
beating together. Soon
there will be many songs
lifted up in the night.

IV

The bride of light emerges
out of night
as we rebuild the bridge
between brother and brother,
as we cross over separation
and exorcise fear.
Her vision manifests in the minds
who meet in her name,
and is grounded in the earth
that nurtures and sustains us.
Through her we learn
to be gentle with ourselves
and with each other.
Through Her we learn to dwell

in the heart
of all things.

V

Soon she will come,
radiating truth
in the four directions,
making medicine
for aching hearts,
teaching the ways of water
and wind.
She will come
to repair the inner temple,
desecrated by
impatience and greed,
defiled by
the economy of fear.

She will come
not as my mother
nor my daughter,
not as my lover,
but as my friend,
my silent companion.
She will be in my eyes
as I look upon the world,
in my hands as I touch
the bodies

of those who love me,
and in my feet
as I venture forth
in the early morning light.

Here, Now, for a Moment

The intensity with which you
are with me
is awesome. It would fill
the deepest hole in me
if I would let it sink
all the way in.

Yet I am not sure I want to be
filled to the brim.
I have worked hard to secure
this emptiness.
I am not so sure my songs
will echo in a well
that is full up.

In moments empty of thought
the marsh is calm.
There is a deep stillness
in the morning mist.
Perhaps we cannot help
looking toward each other
for fulfillment,
yet no matter how much we give
something remains
that cannot be filled.

Our lives ride in that emptiness,
in the revelation of
the moment, as the pine tree
outside my house
rocks in the wind
or as the wind
rushes through the marsh
carrying the crows aloft.

In that emptiness, my friend
leaves her body, yet remains
in heart-communion with me.
I would feel you in the same way,
not from my need for you,
but from my understanding
and appreciation for your beauty.

Today, I am ecstatic in my treetop perch
in the mid-day sun,
thinking of you and my friend,
and knowing that I am
where I need to be,
centered between the sudden
greeting of a robin,
and the fluttering
of newborn leaves.

Available Light

I

In the heart's darkness
light is small.
It barely radiates
at all.

The light we see
in other bodies
casts a shadow
on the wall of self

and the passion play
begins.   Light
is seen without
and darkness wins
within.

II

The inner light
is constant,
but our awareness of it
changes.

The more invested we are
in form,
the less aware we are

of the breath
that sustains it.

And as the breath
is forgotten, shadows cross the mind,
like clouds
over a river.

III

We have tried living
in the double-depth
where shadows cross.
There, in changing light,
we have tried to make
our home. Yet,
being unable to fly,
we could not use our disconnection
with the ground
for any purpose.

IV

We are in the cocoon
dreaming of wings.
Unable to crawl.
Unable to cry out in despair.
Posted beyond fear
to the next step of our journey,
living without wings,

in the consciousness
that gives birth to wings.

V

Now shadows dance
in and out
of sudden patches
of light,
and objects
lose their solidity.
Rainbow wings
are gathered here
in the darkness
where shadows dance
and light sings
under the leaves.

VI

Light is available to us
at all times,
but we see only
what we are willing to see.
In time, the shadow
is gathered in
and the whole self embraced.
Until then,
each sees in the other
the part of himself

he cannot embrace.
Until then,
each tries in desperation
to fill his emptiness
through the other,
but that emptiness
is an illusion,
and the object filling it
is also an illusion.

VII

In true relationship
there is no object consciousness.
Only the light of Self
is seen.
Darkness has disappeared
within and without.
Only the inner light
is manifest, without consequence,
steady, eternal.
It seems fragile only because
it does not display itself,
but it is not fragile.
Opening beyond bias or habit,
It is the power behind
all things.

Another Parting

I

Now you are gone,
traveling the winnow of seasons,
leaving the leaves behind
with wind and snow,
gathering mysterious light
at each crossroads
where the edges are illumined
and the pages of this book
turn from darkness to light
and back again
as the heart ages in many bodies.

Even in this life,
the seasons conspire
to awaken in us
that buried spark of being,
that light which weathers endings,
shedding each layer of form
that has grown too tight
to contain what is within.

II

The weather we know
is but a reflection

of our changing thoughts.
But the heart has
no such boundaries,
only layer upon layer
of responsive being, each emerging
as the moon passes through
the thin gauze of clouds
into the deep blue solitude
of evening.

The weather of the heart
overturns thought, uncovering
a lucid aloneness
like ice falls that glisten
on sheer edges of rock
or birch trees
that arch
like white running deer
in the distance.

IV

The tragedy of consciousness
is not what we know
or do not know,
but what we forget
and have to remember
gradually, entering
another cycle
that begins in the dark

and feeling the rays of light
ripple through the mind like fingers reflected
in a pool of water
someone has stirred.

Yes, we have all been here before.
We were simply overwhelmed
by light
and shut our eyes
for an instant.

What we missed then
passes before us now
and only the heart hears
the repeating footsteps
and knows this play
of light and shadow
is merely another phase
of the god or goddess
we have not yet learned
to love.

If we could be as receptive now
as we will be then,
we too would shudder
at this first touch of dawn,
for there are so many lives wavering
between sunlight and shadow,
between yesterday and today.

Earthquake

for Patricia Sun

We are all so anxious
to set boundaries,
to gesture against
the law of supply.

What is possible
eludes the practiced eye,
abides beside
an unnoticed aloneness.

Living homeless brings
a luminous focus
to all that does not fit
some inner purpose.

Others seem on the edge,
as though their lives
are too small
to hold the contents,

as if at any moment
death could walk in
and strike a better deal
than the one

so tentatively upheld.
My own world seems
full of holes that widen
with every action

or reaction. It doesn't
seem to matter what I do.
Each day intention swells
and contracts,

leaving deeper gaps
for light to fill, braving
the darkest crannies
of my invented self,

and showing me again and again
that there is nothing there
except beliefs
that create and destroy

boundaries. It is peculiar
to feel how much pain
is stored in the body
just because we want

something different
from what we have,
or to feel how easy
things become

when the pain rises,
and the body trembles
uncontrollably, or how
even thoughts cease

when light takes over.
I guess I'm beginning
to understand why my chair
began to shake

when you made your sounds
--your voice creating
a vibratory screen
around my body

as if to show me how much
I was holding in.
When you stopped singing,
the boundaries were gone

and the inner hardness
lifted up with wings,
and I watched that otherness
enter the sky

like an albatross
no longer betrayed, leaving me
vulnerable and empty. I felt
as a mother must feel

when her belly has opened
and what was, is no longer hers,
or as the earth must feel
after its bowels move,

darkening the sky
and signalling her displaced children
to end their stumbling search
and return home.

Point of Stillness

I

I have found that point of stillness
lying next to you,
a fire that begins long and burning in the body,
dissolving skin, heart, hands and lips
into a sound as of wings.

Now I feel you but cannot touch you.
The fire in my hands is pressed to space,
a burning emptiness, a love orphaned
and alone.

I was told that we must pass through this place
on our way to an ecstasy
which is without form.

II

We were joined in an ancient place.
From there, I came as water and became wood.
You came as wind and became stone.
Tomorrow, out of our discarded bodies,
they will make wooden fences and stone walls.
Grass will grow out from our pores,
and blood will cut a gravely channel
down the hill, pooling
at the entrance to our ears.

Lovers will hear the echo of our footsteps
in the places where they meet.
We will carry willow blossoms and thorns
to the marriage bed and the altar,
and the rain will disguise the sound
of our voices.

Do you remember the time we journeyed north
and I left a trail of blood on the snow,
and you sat there weeping?

III

Are we one body or two? One movement
or many movements collapsed into one?
Are we the dream or the one to whom
the dream comes?

I remember your breath
moving across my body
as the clouds move across the sky,
looking for forgotten children
in the lake below.

In your presence,
light gathered at the eyelids
and a gentle ecstasy opened
at the fingertips
and the soles of the feet.

Now your hands move across me
like leaves driven in the wind.

Soon the snow will arrive
and you will come looking for me
under four foot drifts,
but you will not find me.

IV

You do not manage the world very well,
nor do I.
Each of us has gone where s/he can be consoled.
We are not strong enough
to surrender
to what our hearts already know.

Two halves of the same coin trying to meet:
how else
do you explain it?

V

You whom I love effortlessly,
without desire,
(for desire is only wanting
what one does not have)
with you I have felt the eternal fire
entering the heart at the point of stillness,
where bodies begin and end
and nothing of the world
can come between us.

A December Morning

It is dawn.
Snow lightly grips the marsh,
and clouds close
the horizon
in.
Silence reigns.
Boughs
of pine and holly
catch the snow
and offer it back
as a gift.

They are not
spring fed
like the maple or birch,
ablaze
before the rift
that left them
stark in falling snow:
beauty's
solitary witnesses.

Now the quickener
spins his web
underground
where Demeter's daughter
lies.

In her hands
she hides
a hidden faith
while her mother moves
through stormy skies
like a wraith
caught between
two worlds.

Her grief
holds back the surge
of light
and spring cannot emerge
until she lets
the daughter go. I abide with the Mother
in small increments
becoming increasingly
emotional
as tears
run down my cheeks
and ecstatic sounds
fly like fingers
of estranged light
into my heart.

It is dawn.
Snow lightly grips the marsh
and hidden sounds
echo from hill to hill
across the frozen ground.

This is a chorale
fantasy
for solo piano
and the lone gull
a phoenix
spinning and diving
in the snow.

Toward The Edge of Light
for Vincent

I

The boatswain's oar
dipped
to silence
and you
or I
just another survivor
gripping the top
of the skiff,
pulling himself out of
the cold, clammy waters,
surveying shores peopled by savages
living in a time
before paper songs
betrayed them: red bodies in the mist
by harbor's entrance
canoes skipping through the dark waves
under dome of moonlight,
painted bodies not yet baptized
in the blood of the cross
nor bathed in tides of addiction
beyond their understanding
or control.

This is the fulcrum, this place
where dreams cross
revealing the sound of our own wings
beating in the silences
between the cawing of gulls,
our only tool to negotiate
a damaged world
where hopes are bred from ashes,
and voices strewn and buried
in a bludgeoning wind
like the one at
Auschwitz
or Hiroshima.

It is strange consolation
knowing this is the bitter end
of the hegemony of fear,
knowing that only a cryptic music
hidden in the thymus
will unlock these jammed gears
racing toward Armageddon.

II

Looking seaward from Braces Cove
toward that pale stuttering light
on the eastern horizon,
you hear the swash of boats far off
the rumbling of waves

not yet brought to shore,
a humming in the ear
like the sound of a jew's harp
or distant bell buoy - soliloquy
to the sands of beaches
nearby and far away.

Whoever hears this sound
sooner or later
uses it to enter uncharted places,
nuances still held by water,
wind, and sky.
Yet, you wonder and so do I
who will give us
a loaf of bread for this occasion,
or a bottle of wine to sip at sea.

III

Working with the heart
is dangerous.
There are casualties.
Families reel as wounds surface.
There is no polite confusion,
but, as in a dream,
sudden ineffable movements
to where the energy
is most intense.

The child cannot forget.
He spends his life
remembering
the moment of abandonment.
His boundaries are violated
again and again by lovers
perceived as parents.
There is no safety here,
and what solace there is
comes from strangers
who happen to be passing through.

IV

Years ago I sat across from you
fastened to a vigil
not of letters.

Out of the immense loneliness
of your journey,
I watched you carry in a broken bucket
the water of your soul,
bathing your wounds
in the moonlight.

The success you courted never came,
and isolation seemed to be
the price of your freedom,
yet you did not quit.

The tears of the poet
water the garden
where joy has its fragile bloom.
They gather where hope
is concealed
and sadness lingers.

From them come the first
trembling words,
the first dim rays of light
muscled out of the darkness.

V

It is cold in the shop at night
though the heat is on,
and you arise from dreams
with the smell of death on your hands
wondering who gave you the knife
to cut the cord
linking the past to this place,
moving with difficulty
from minor to major key,
like an out of tune violin
or black crow's cry, poignant
yet heavy with darkness.

Out of the homeless arms of night,
the hidden light
is cast adrift

and bellies up in bodies
hunched over in doorways,
the hidden limbs of Christ sitting up out of night
dawn eyed and hungry
or released to bioways
hundreds of feet in the sky
where men and women in suits
prepare summons and foreclosure notices,
pages of graceless litany
flying off laser printers
or lost in a computer file no one can find.

Out of the eclipse of night
the silver thread of light
slips by death's narrow fingers,
as breath by breath the mind is linked
to the objects of desire,
fastening itself to the tides
of greed, anger, and remorse,
while somewhere
in the black spaces of the mind
widows still scan the harbor
awaiting unsung captains lost at sea.

Only by the boatswain's oar
can time by appropriately measured:
and from the building of the pyramids
to this equally labored moment
is just one wink of Shiva's eye.

VI

I admit to you, I have strayed
far enough from the music
of the heart
to require debriefing
from the logic of threat and counter threat,
fished free of the cacophony
of insidious thoughts,
premature judgments and petty jealousies,
broken out of polite hiding
and brought face to face
with marketplace economies
and their unsavory byproducts: raw sewerage
on the beaches,
heroin needles mutinied at sea.

All this
for services rendered.

VII

By the sad-eyed light of day's end
we return, the refugees
of time: minds bruised, bodies tense
as crossed wires,
hundreds of thousands of us
jamming the streets and subways.
If you look closely, you can see

it is all a dream
of self-incarceration,
a subtle death wish
denying hope and responsibility
which cannot be split,
a schizophrenia of the nerves
in the grip of fear.

Yet to reverse the collective impulse
toward self-destruction
is not as hard as we think. You showed me that.
I have only to be who I am,
to move with the moon's blessing
over these quickening waters.
Listen carefully and you will hear
a thin sound of oars
in the lifting fog,
moving eastward
toward the edge of light.

Forgiveness

I don't want to wait till your funeral or mine
to meet you again.

Ego is just the superficial part
of you or me.
What is deeper has the same authority
and cannot disagree.

You and I must both learn to share
this house of cards,
regardless of the hand we've been dealt.

Every ego is baked
in the flames of its own desire
and made to stand watch
over the soul's journey
to shores it will never see.

We do not need to sentence each other,
but to help lighten the load.

Like anything else, money has
only the significance one gives to it.

Now I am in this opera and so are you,
but you don't like the baritone part,

because you can't compete with it.
The answer is not to try. Each voice is heard
when its aria comes.

Next to that greatness, what am I or you?
Why not help me bury the bone so deep
the dog of shame cannot find it.

If I attack, do not defend,
nor take offense,
for I can only hurt myself
and then I need your help
to undo what I have done.

My attack on you is merely
the judgment I have laid against myself,
which your defenselessness
enables me to see.

If we forgive as often as we blunder
our burden cannot be heavy,
nor can we refuse to see the light
that dwells within us equally.

It is not for the sake of the ego
but for the sake of the soul
that we meet. That we understood
in our hearts many years ago.

Estuary

I

By the bridge where the waters
of the North and South rivers meet,
a scavenger circles his prey,
floating down from the sky
in a funnel of descending arcs.

This is our heritage, this dance of death
unheralded, obscure, intense
but only for a moment.

Surrounded on one side
by this confluence of rivers,
and on the other by the ocean,
the outer reach of land
yields inch by inch to the tides,
or suddenly
as it did one night up shore,
when a nor'easter tore at the land's thigh
cutting a new channel for water
to enter.

It is not just this vulnerable promontory
that is gripped by the watery assault.
Even further inland where rivers begin
as underground streams

and swales catch the spring rains,
you can feel the subtle wound of water
as it trickles out of the ground
into hundreds of tiny brooks,
feeding down to the sea.

The grip of water on land is fierce.
It brings the blood up in the loins
and carries our bodies away.

This edge of land has seen many storms.
Men have met their deaths
climbing endless ladders of water,
and women have waited
wrinkled and brittle,
thirsting in vain for a single kiss,
as the faces of their lovers
no longer bound by flesh
haunt the ivory bones
that turn beneath the sea.

I watch now at this edge of rock
where the buoy sings in the deep fog
and the harbor groans like a halyard in the wind
counting its missing daughters and sons.

II

We worship civilization's blunt edge,

tools that bludgeon when they should cut,
ideas bought and sold on the 6 o'clock news;
every week a new angle on suffering and sin,
for whatever one mind can imagine
another will enact.

Life is as cheap as a gun worn at the hip.
You may say it is only for show,
yet bodies occasionally fall
on the dung stained streets
and the smell of blood
mixes with the smell of anisette and espresso
coming from the bakeries and cafes.

The captains of cocaine
feed the children of pain,
battered, stolen, or molested,
while corporate trash makes babies for cash,
conceived in absentia
and grown in rented wombs.

And while the inmates of suburbia
recoil from the outstretched hands
of the homeless
one crazy old lady
neither nervous nor distraught
roams the neighborhoods
making lists of her victims.

We fear the untamed phantasies of the powerless.
We who gave them the gun of rejection
can hardly be surprised
when they take it out of their mouths
and point it at us.

I awake in the night to the screams
of children hit by bullets.
I see their gentle faces torn and bleeding
and the empty expression on the face
of their frail assassin.

Like Raskolnikov,
I relive the images of violation
over and over again,
yet I have killed no one.
Still I am responsible. I can't deny it.

Long after midnight the lightning strikes,
bringing down a deluge of water and sound,
the house shaking like a wayward ark
about to set sail over the flooded marsh.

III

After the making of meaning,
after the seed and its search,
after the wish and its fulfillment,
comes greed,

the unending desire for something
other than what is,
something that only briefly satisfies
before we begin to crave
something new.

Here, under the heavens
the river is cool and silent.
Shadows move across it at every bend.
Its journey is serpentine,
yet it has nothing to hide.
It merely objects to a detailed agenda,
to a psychology of straight lines.
Following the river gives you perspective.
You see the marsh hills
from every vantage point
and move on, knowing that it will take
a long time to get home.
Speedboats are awkward here,
and planes cast long but brief shadows.
Their passengers don't seem to understand
that nothing here is quickly deciphered.

If we would serve our Mother well,
we must understand her anger
and her caress, her sudden changes
and her deep mystery.

IV

Each day we eat from the hand of the serpent,
giving the mind work, giving the world sin.
And each day wrong becomes right
because it is easy to achieve,
and right becomes wrong
because it demands more
than we are prepared to give.
From the garden,
where life is effortless and eternal,
to exile in the world,
where life is defined by death,
and procreation and birth is of the body,
from Eden to Sodom in a single breath,
a single attempt to take power
when power is already available and in place,
from the power of trust to the power of choice,
from being to doing,
from innocence to intention,
we come, choosing what we desire
but cannot understand
instead of what we understand without desiring,
reaching for the fruit of passion
which leads to death
instead of the fruit of Tao
which leads beyond life and death
to the very door of Creation. There
the myriad things are given impetus and shape,
there in the dark eternal,

which is neither dark nor light,
in the womb of silence, in the bodiless arms
of our Mother.

V

Joy is found in the abandonment of thought.
A mind which moves like a stallion
across unfenced fields
is a mind that sings
and brings breath back into the body.

No, the descendants of Urizen
shall not prevail against nature.
What is of Creation
must be redeemed from Experience.
Innocence is not lost, but hides
in thunder and wind, in the stillness
of the mountains, and the rhythm of the sea.

It is there behind the strain of the face
locked in defensiveness or disbelief.
It is there on the underside of the eyelids,
in the male and female channels of the nose.
It is there in the arms lifted up to the sky
or in the back bent toward the ground.

It is there wherever energy flows.
And if it does not flow in the body,
then mind cannot reclaim it,

and if it does not flow in the mind,
then Spirit cannot arise there, bringing each life
into harmony with nature,
and thereby harnessing it
to do the Lord's work.

VI

It is agreed.
We will gather at the appropriate time
at a place we cannot anticipate
but will recognize when we arrive.
We will draw from resources
we do not now know that we have
as help arrives without asking.
For we are the vine, laden with fruit.
We are the choice we were afraid to make,
and we are making it now,
giving up our preoccupation with good and evil,
so that we can be a channel for life,
for breath is no longer in short supply
nor does equality have any measure.
As with me, so with you;
as with us, so with others.
This is the blessing of the saint of life,
crucified upon the crossed branches
of the tree of good and evil.

VII

River of stillness, where two become one again.
River of thought brought to the harvest of love.
River cutting through the dry, pasty ground.
You who make the dust into mud for planting.
Nothing terrifies like a dry world.
Famine lives in the hot sun
and scavengers circle overhead.

You who made ground for us to pass over
from the waters of the Red Sea,
make water from this dust
so that the seed dies not on the ground,
so that our children taste
the dew on their salt lips,
so that the branches of the tree may be uplifted
and offer us shade and solace,
so that the dry, shriveled bird, looking for shade
in the thin shadow of a fencepost,
may remember how to fly.

Forgive us, though we need not be forgiven.
Love us, though we cannot understand
what love means.
Remember us, though we cannot
ourselves remember
where we came from,
or where we were going

when the rays of the sun arrested us
and held the planet hostage
for a single drop of rain.

Life that does not contain death cannot live,
and land without water means certain death.
From death, life emerges
with water for the parched ground,
and from our ancestor's bones
we must once again learn to fashion
instruments for writing, planting,
painting, and drumming. The tradition
must be carried on so that it is remembered well
before the moment of death. The tradition
must be handed down.

VIII

Mind of water. Mind of life.
Kneel now at the moment of the sacrament.
Many teachings there are, but only One Truth,
many teachers but only one subject.
And the subject shall object to no one,
and the object shall become subject again,
as he or she who for the first time
survives the fire of infatuation
or the sting of blame. Kneel now
at the moment of Truth, for she has arrived,
Mother of us all, she who is wordless
in listening, and without thought

in receiving us into her arms,
long forgotten, long disbelieved.

IX

Forgive us, Mother
for we have sinned against you
and against ourselves.
We have built skyscrapers
on the old Indian burial grounds.
Rivers of asphalt now divide
the ancestral lands.

Sodom has been rebuilt;
Babylon reinhabited. But the rains will come
after the heat abates;
yes, the rains will come
hauling these statues of salt
down to the sea.

Then we will build our boats from trees again
in a land without cities.
Then we will come here
as the Wampanoag did
to walk and swim on the beach
and fish in the tidepools of this estuary
where the river of the past
meets the river of the future,
where life and death meet
and merge into the sea.

The Hands of God

The Aids babies
bone thin, with muscles
barely able
to raise a smile
reach for the hands
held out to them
and look deeply
into the eyes that meet theirs
without fear.

Nobody said love would be easy.
The nurse has just buried
her fifth baby this week.
She no longer believes
that God
loves these children.

To Brother Toby,
every moment is precious,
and every child deserves
this little ransom of love
at the edge of death.

He does not come to justify God
or explain
why these children suffer,
but to look and to touch,
to be an instrument of love
in a world of pain.

God is absent in human affairs
until one man or woman
rises up to give
the love that is needed.
Without that gesture,
the world trembles in its misery,
and God stands speechless
before our pain.

Love's pathway in this world
is through our hearts and minds,
and fear always blocks
its way, our fear
that we are unworthy,
or that our brother is unworthy,
or that God is absent
in our time of need.

In the Aids wards of Romania,
hundreds of children die each week.
There, the face of pain
is solemn, almost resigned.
To most of these children,
death is a welcome friend,
and its hands are softer
than the hands of life.

But to a few, something deeper
has come, something
that cannot be told in words,
but can be seen in the eyes
of those whose bodies
have been held and caressed.

They alone are God's witnesses.

Brought Back to Love
for Pepi

I suffer for the pain of the world, stripped
of laughter, left to its own solitary
illusions, for the voices
shallow with fear,
and the hands too quick for the body.

I suffer for the twisted acts
greeting us through a doorway:
this sudden warmth of blood
burning in my lap
like a candle in a house of prayer.

I, Pepi Ferrini, have left this place
at the hands of desperate young men
who could not understand
the laughter in my body
nor the tide that must release it
to the world.

Now they have taken one step further
into their pain.
They have turned the corner
on their loved ones.

Even their prayers are broken with my blood,
and each night for the rest of their lives

they must sleep with the body
I have left behind.

Who has been robbed, I ask you?

I suffer for the pain of this world,
for the gift they were not patient enough
to receive. As a boy, it was given to me
as I walked these downtrodden streets.
I saw it in the faces
of some of the old people, aging
quicker than the land, their skin
wrinkled by the salt air,
their hearts like mended sails
singing in the wind.

It was a kind of pride in our dignity
mixed with a great vulnerability.
It kept us going, and helped us
laugh at ourselves. We learned
to drink and dance,
and tease the women, glad to have each other
because we all knew how deep
our aloneness was.

I wanted to give them that gift,
because I knew their tears
were no different from mine.
I wanted to help them loosen up,

but they were too impatient.
They were afraid of me.
They were afraid to be vulnerable.

I understand. And you must too.
Even this violation of us must be brought back
to innocence. Even this reckless
and unnecessary suffering must be
brought back to love.

Remember, each of us comes to his time,
and no matter how it comes to him,
he doesn't protest, but goes as gracefully
as he can, using the gift he has been given
to navigate the silent waters
beyond the body, where
the voices of the old people he knew
are calling to him, so near
and yet so far away.

I understand your grief, for it is mine too.
We must go through it, all of us together.
It is our last voyage.
When it is over, the gift I have
will be yours too,
and you will know that it was never mine
to begin with.

I leave you with a vision of the people dancing.
The salt wind is drying their tears,

and laughter is in their hearts.
They are turning the grapes
to wine. They are moving their feet
and clapping their hands.
I am feeling so good to be amongst them.

Illuminations

I

Each moment
contains all that manifests
before or after it.

II

A man becomes bound,
not to the objects of the world,
but to his expectations of himself
in relation to them.

This is an predicament
few escape.

III

Only when we are divided
do we pause to consider
what path to choose.

IV

The Self is a wilderness.
There is no way into It
or out of It.

V

It is hard to understand perfection
when each of us takes from life
only what he is willing to receive.

VI

Things always become
even for a moment
as we expect them to be.

VII

We all continue to lick our wounds
long after the scar tissue
has formed above them.

VIII

You find reflected in others
only the beauty you perceive
in yourself.

IX

The grey clouds are edged
by the sunlight
tucked inside them.

X

Everything is the Self
split into different bodies,
different motions of energy
held together instant to instant
by my gaze.

XI

Nature spares only
what was never hers to give.

XII

Life is a sieve:
only the Real passes through.

XIII

I seek what is not transferable,
what runs shy of any deed
and rules before thought begins.

XIV

Each expectation
betrays our infinite embrace,
closing us into that space
where bodies meet
and come asunder.

XV

Truth tolerates no subtraction.
Everything we have
must be used.

XVI

Changing prisons hold the light,
and we inevitably hold on too tight
to the forms we must leave behind.

XVII

Love is like the rain
touching us everywhere at once
with the same mysterious hands.

XVIII

An open heart
renews the continuity
of all things.

XIX

Those who seek money ask for it,
instead of passing their gift on
to those who have waited patiently
to receive it.

XX

Any meaning I give to my life
is not the one it has.

XXI

Nature never allows closure,
nor the manipulation
of things into place.

XXII

Those who are patient and loving
always arrive in time
to pick the fruits.

XXIII

Sometimes what we think we know
is exactly what interferes
with our understanding.

XXIV

Every mistake we make
is an opportunity
to separate what we are
from what we are not.

XXV

We think who we are,
but we are not
who we think we are.

XXVI

Every time I try
to find love outside myself,
I am drawn out to sea,
or stranded like a crab
at low tide on the beach.

XXVII

My premature commitments
remind me of misgivings
I blindly chose to overlook.

XXVIII

I no long wonder why people
do not keep their promises.
Their words reflect changing minds,
boats bearing with waves
and weather, without anchor
in a deeper source.

XXIX

When the density of fear
attenuates,
our hands lift the fog.

XXX

Each day the world begins
flooded with light.

XXXI

In spite of the beauty of houses
framed by hands, set plumb
into a place of fierce energy,
where the sun rests
on the edge of a cloud
like an eye about to open,
it is not easy to suffer the land.
The body is not the same;
the mind must be mended;
the spirit must dwell in a different way.

XXXII

After thousands of heavy,
disconsolate sounds,
this silence is like holy water
and my body a boat that puts out to sea
without oar or sail.

XXXIII

Light anticipates
more than our eyes can see.

XXXIV

A false shadow weighs
on my breath.

Beneath the pure song
of the birds,
the image is grainy
and the dream ends
without any sensation
of waking.

I do not know where I am
anymore.

XXXV

There are sea squalls
in the heart,
and moments becalmed
when the wind barely moves
and even the breath
falters.

XXXVI

Nothing is what it seems.
Only the snow is real,
falling steadily
in the silence
that is always there,
but not felt or seen
till the snow comes
to cover it over.

XXXVII

I do not need a lot any more.
I have run myself ragged seeking more.
Living in the heart, even for a moment,
where the rain falls, softening the air,
I am satisfied with a single bird call
sharply pronounced under this canopy
of clouds and budding leaves.

XXXVIII

Centering the Universe
inside the Self
brings direct perception
of Being.

There are no exaggerations,
no interrupted moments.

XXXIX

Above the trivia of mind,
there is a complete
and welcome silence.
Hills rise above the misty marsh.
Magnolia and dogwood trees bloom
outside my front door.

XL

Sometimes looking at things
in detail
can be exhausting
and unnecessary.
Focusing too intensely
objectifies Being
and robs it
of its spontaneity
and grace.

XLI

It is important
to think things through completely
before attempting
to explain them to others.

XLII

In nature, there is one simple rule:
the more you resist,
the larger the enemy looms;
the more you want,
the larger the unbefriended room
inside the heart.

XLIII

At dusk
even the longest and whitest of boats
fades into the darkness of water and sky.

XLIV

Voice of spring:
"I am the voice of ascending energy,
rooted in the ground,
reaching for the heavens."

Voice of autumn:
"I am the voice of descending energy,
leaves aflutter in the wind,
roots bracing for winter."

XLV

I am the wind in the flesh
of the bird
before he takes off
from the cliff.

I am his anticipation,
as he releases the branch,
and the sudden rise of warmth
within, as he sails out
over the gorge.

I am the wind in the flesh
of the bird
as he alights
on a large rock below.

I am his ever-so-slight
sense of completion,
the ending of that moment
in time,
whether or not it occurs again.

XLVI

The hills dip and slide
here in the marsh
where river meets the sea.

Fog settles in above the treetops;
stars are hidden;
and you can hear the ocean,
though you cannot see it.

Night unfolds
with an impersonality
measured only by
the horn of the bell buoy
as it rolls
on the slippery breast
of the sea.

XLVII

Not needing to change what is,
nor resisting change if it comes of itself,
this is what it means to dwell
in the heart.

XLVIII

Cold grips the early morning,
the sky chisel sharp blue
against the white buildings
steepled and leaning out of night.

The body bristles, goosebumps on the skin,
and the lungs ache on the inhale.
There is a nakedness here
tucked away from any purpose,
a sharp fender of trust, askew
on the shabby body of time.

Like a potter,
I work on the wheel of mind,
turning shapes that scatter
across the field of memory
like leaves across the pavement,
hesitant, unpredictable, sudden.

Winter Landscape

Without sufficient love,
the branches,
bled back bare for winter,
stare with eyes closed,
and anxious boats groan
in the icy waters of the harbor.

Without sufficient love,
the unity of night retreats
along these winding
seatown streets
and night dissolves
into hundreds of torn roses.

Without sufficient love,
dawn arrives
thick inside the throats
of newborn birds
and air has the weight
of solitary voices.

Blessing the Fleet

The Sanctuary at Rock Harbor

I am the one forgotten
and betrayed, the infant son
left to a harvest
of confusion and tears;
once shamed, but blameless now,
lingering in the garden
where the lion lies
with the lamb
and dark clouds gather overhead.

In this sanctuary
alive with the breath
of raindrops and flowers,
where boats put out to sea
under a thin canopy
hiding stars, I heard Him
crying out in self-pity
and despair, but now I know
the voice belongs to me.

I am the one who has strayed.
And I am the one returning now.

The Messenger

I am a messenger of the infinite mind.
I come before you as a friend,
a brother.
I recall you to yourself.
I recall you to God.

I do not make promises. My presence
is its own promise.
I come to you to reveal
what fear has covered up.
I come to affirm what is Real.

I do not speak of the past
or the future.
The kingdom is now.
Today, this very moment,
we have arrived.

You are all members of my family.
My family has no end.
I go out to all who would receive me,
and I am sustained by
your love and gratitude.

My love does not criticize,
nor does it pamper you. It dares you
to be who you are.

It dares you to throw off your chains
of blame and self-pity.

It empowers you to create your life
with energy and trust.
My message is a simple one.
You are loved. I love you.
Your brothers and sisters love you.

We are all hands of God
afraid to touch, afraid to ask
for affection, learning
that love is the only blessing
we can give each other.

The infinite mind has no fears
or regrets. Its messenger
sees beauty in every form,
truth in every face,
love in every heart.

Nothing is wasted.
Nothing is in short supply.
What is real remains real
and what is false remains false.
Truth is self-evident.

Prologue

I

I stretch out now like the breath
or the dim colors of dawn
curlicued in the haze.
I am the ground on which you move
and the ladders of thought
on which you climb.

Mine is the watery path of light
that moves with the observer.
That is why
there is that distance
between the will and the eye,
that pause at the horizon
where water meets sky,
and unseen ladders
empty into unreachable mist.

Breath by breath I bring the myriad forms
into being, joining one
to the throat of the breaking surf
and another to a gull's solitary cry,
each a link in a chain of wanderers
celebrating dawn.

II

I am the weather of your heart,
laboring for balance.
I am the rain
entering you with open eyes,
and the clouds grazing your skin,
keeping your shadows
locked within.

Repeatedly, I open you up
and seal you in,
conspiring with sun and wind
to remove the shadows from your bodies
painlessly, and without even
a trace of longing.

III

You are not guilty of anything except self-abuse,
nor are your mistakes due to ignorance
but to pride,
to your refusal to cooperate
with the intelligence that guides you
out of the mechanics of thought
into the space of surrender.
Between the language of need
and the language of touch,
you stand alone,

yearning for the rain that has already fallen
between your fingers.

IV

If you want to receive me,
stop pretending that I am not with you.

V

I am the wind in the mind of the dreamer
and the dream that dissolves
in the wind.

I am the house you enter
when fear leaves
and loneliness troubles
no longer.

Don't Uphold the World

I

Don't uphold the world.
Let it go where it will.
You do not have to go with it
or try to make it go with you.

The world has nothing to do
with who you are.
It appears substantial
only because you
entertain it.

The world is the projection
of illusory images
upheld by the thought
that you
are separate from me.

In this thought is death born
and life made private
to compete for love.

II

In each moment, we make the world
or let it go.

In each moment, we fear death
or welcome unconditional love.

Only a quiet mind can release itself to love.
Minds that labor
separate the seam of life
crippling each moment that offers a bridge
to acceptance and peace.

The world of separation
seems so solid
yet it too runs its course
and death recycles
what it upholds.

Knowing this, how can you struggle,
pushing one person away
or pulling another toward you?
Minds that are joined cannot be torn apart
or manipulated into place.

For love is eternal.
It is ever present.
It cannot be taken away from you
and given to someone else.
Whoever withholds love
keeps it from himself.
Whoever gives it
gains the recognition

of what he is
and has always been.

III

A single moment of peace
is worth more
than a lifetime of struggle.
Beliefs that do not support peace
uphold the world
and tear the seam of unity
between brothers.

These beliefs
run between pain and sadness
like a thief looking
for a safe place to hide.
They are all too visible.

Yet reparation can be made
through release.
For nothing
has been stolen,
only the idea of stealing
remains.

IV

Forgiveness runs like a clear stream
between eyes that see
equally.

All is movement and grace,
because nothing is held to where it
had been.

When life finds this freedom,
death has nothing to do
but watch.

Song of the Christchild

The world comes into being
and passes away.

But I do not come into being
or pass away.

I have always been here.
I have never been anywhere else.

I am the world's creator.
I am its destroyer.

I preserve its ministries
or let them die in the wind.

I am freedom and bondage,
hope and despair.

It is all my doing.
It is all my undoing.

When I am absent
you seek me.

When I am present
you overlook me.

In this way alone
are my comings and goings proclaimed.

Fathers and Sons

I

I tried to find my father
in his brother,
but it did not work.
There are no substitute fathers.

His brother
tried to love me as a father,
but he couldn't be any more father to me
than he could be to his own son.

I had to go looking for my father.
I had to forgive him
for not being there for me
the way I needed him to be.

I had to remove the separation from him
in my heart;
I had to stop my acquiescence
to his carefully kept distance.

I had to move into the space
left by his retreat
and ask
for what he found difficult to give.

II

The child has no choice but to ask for love,
nor can he have any explanation
for his failure to receive it
other than his own unworthiness.

The adult looks across face to face.
He sees the fear the father feels
and forgives the father
and forgives himself

so that he does not carry the fear
and the feelings of unworthiness
to his own children.

It was hard to find my father.
I had to let the past go
and meet him in the present.
When I did, I found him also
reaching out to me.

Healing always flows both ways.

III

My son is lonely.
He wants to be with me.
He does not know how to say this.

In my absence,
he has too much of his mother,
and not enough of me.

My daughter is angry.
She feels close to me,
but doesn't trust it,
because I go away.
Thus, the family pattern
asserts itself again:
the men unable to deal with the emotional demands
of family life
withdrawing from their wives
and children.

Having found my father,
I must learn to be one.
I must learn to embrace my son
in his loneliness
and my daughter in her anger.

They feel abandoned.
It was never my intention
to abandon them.
It was never my father's intention
to abandon me.

Yet the loss to both of us
is real.

There is great sadness
in this.

The lineage has been broken.
The daughter has not been loved
and given away.
The son has not been empowered
to trust himself.

Now I re-enter the hearth
with all my vulnerability,
learning just to be
present there.
That is where my wholeness lies.
That is where my ability to parent lies.

IV

No, we are not perfect,
nor do we have to be.
We do not have to be afraid
of our pain
or our vulnerability.
We have been afraid too long.
We have pretended too long
to be strong.
It is time that we witnessed
to our pain.
There is a grief here so deep
we do not know where we begin and it ends.

We cannot find its place of origin alone.
We need to help each other do that.

So we come forward gently
to regain the energy of the heart.
We meet as not as competitors,
but as equals, with compassion
for one another.
As fathers, we reclaim our sons.
As sons, we embrace our fathers.

Thus is the lineage reconstructed
so that the love of men
will not die from the earth,
but be born anew,
in gentleness and strength.

Promises

I

Some men make promises to the Holy One.
They alone understand.
Each day the promise must be renewed.
Each day it must be tested
in the flame of aloneness.

II

Do not forget, you who would live out
your yearning with another,
do not forget that leaving has the same sudden steps,
the same aftermath of inertia.

Pray to the sun for sustenance,
for the rays of sunlight touch all things,
and there are endless suns
within the sun we know.

Do not pray to the moon,
but do penance beneath her cold rays,
for her changing light is fed by tears,
and her fullness is as sharp as her absence.

Do not make promises under the moon
until you have learned to love all of her phases,
for she is as ruthless as she is gentle,
and her changing weather is but a reflection
of your own changing thoughts.

Dialogue

You say

that we met once before
in a spring without beginning,
that you stood before me
and I did not see you,
that you spoke
and I answered with the sound
of your words echoing
through the empty spaces
of my body. You say
that I declined
to hear the litany
of the rain,
and that when you bowed your head
to show me the wet leaves
clinging to your hair,
I pretended not to see them.

I say

it is hard to watch
the nakedness of the face
emerging from its shell,
hard to feel
the trembling of the scales
touched beyond

the bone. I say
it is hard to meet
with either breath or hands
the inviolable symmetry
of your body.

Morning Snow

It was the most opportune
moment
for the beginning of winter--
the first few
reticent flakes of snow
flecked from the dark folds
of your hair
as you rose half asleep
at two o'clock,
abandoning the closeness
of this narrow bed
for that distance you love
but cannot wholly
abide.

When I came to wake you
at seven,
the flurries were slowly
dispersing the darkness.
"Is it love or the desire to love
that keeps us going?" I asked
as you woke with a twinge
of surprise, skidding
out of the ritual
incongruity
of your dreams
into the bleak snow-webbed
light -- into winter
with all its visible uncertainty.

Phases of Wholeness

Sometimes I wake with only a sliver of the moon
rising above me
and remember how we once lay alone together
looking out at the trees
and barely touching--
an image that endures
beyond all my phantasies of romance
and all my premonitions
of separation,
because it delineates
the fact that you are sometimes more,
sometimes less than
my lover,
and that sometimes
our love comes into focus
when we lose its fullness,
when we understand
how to be generous
with what we cannot share.

Homecoming

I

I have spent many lives approaching you
and moving away,
but it doesn't seem to matter.

My connection to you remains
wherever I go.
It modulates the distance,
expanding and contracting it
at will.

It is the original desire,
traveling back and forth over time,
fastening the soul down from its urgency
to a builder's gait.

Nothing can be accomplished without it.
It has waited like a sleeping child
while the mind
has moved its labyrinthine limbs
through all these detours.

II

Hundreds of women have moved
through the caves

of my heart,
but only one has remained.

I thought you were one of many
in a rite of passage,
leading the animal up into the sunlight,
binding and releasing speech,
but not so.
There has never been a time
when you have not been with me.
There has never been a time
when innocence has strayed
from the body of our bliss.

Whenever we come together,
angelic beings share our bed,
interweaving our embrace
with a steadiness
that threads our dreams.

III

It is their presence I love best,
a hidden tapestry of colors and shapes
from which you emerge
a white wave in the darkness,
a repeating sound,
wanting touch without end,
wanting to embrace life

even as death caresses the shoulders.
It is their shadows that dance
on the windcurled sands,
changing emptiness to unbounded movement,
changing fear
to a sadness that gives birth
to love.

IV

We call it many things to encircle its subtlety,
but it remains beyond our grasp.
Softer, yet more insistent than pain,
it dwells inside us.
It cannot be tampered with.
It comes into being
no matter how much we resist,
no matter how much distance we put
between us.

Paul Ferrini is a writer, teacher and counselor, whose primary focus is the integration of spirituality into daily life. He has written several books on this topic, including *From Ego to Self, Virtues of the Way, A Contemporary Book of Changes, The Body of Truth, Available Light* and *The Bridge to Reality.*

Paul's work centers on Self-empowerment issues. He encourages a heart-centered awareness that deepens our trust and faith, and awakens the potential for healing in our lives. Paul's background blends a study of depth psychology with an investigation of both eastern and western spiritual traditions. He is also a student and teacher of A Course in Miracles.

In 1980, while driving across the Arizona desert, Paul received a new system of numerology, which he developed as a therapeutic tool for accessing our inner guidance. This was the awakening of his channeling ability, which he uses regularly in his writing, teaching and counseling activities.

Paul's professional experience also includes owning his own real estate company, designing/building homes and developing land. While working in education, he edited a national magazine, and directed two nationwide research projects resulting in the books: *Career Change* (1978) and *The Interdependent Community* (1980). He has a Masters Degree from the Antioch Graduate School of Education in New Hampshire and a Bachelor's Degree from Marlboro College in Vermont.